Flowers
of Field and Meadow

Titles in the series:

Clouds and Weather
Butterflies and Moths of Britain and Europe
Garden Birds of Britain and Europe
Conifers of Britain and Europe
Deciduous Trees of Britain and Europe
Beetles of Britain and Europe
Berries of Britain and Europe
Rocks
Flowers of Field and Meadow

Longman Group Limited
Longman House, Burnt Mill, Harlow,
Essex CM20 2JE, England

Originally published in German by
Gräfe und Unzer GmbH, München
© Gräfe und Unzer GmbH, München

English language edition © Longman Group Limited 1986

First published by Longman Group Limited 1986

British Library Cataloguing in Publication Data
Lippert, Wolfgang
Flowers of field and meadow.—(Longman nature guides)
1. Wild flowers—Identification   2. Meadow flora—Identification
I. Title
582.12'0915'3   QK85.5

ISBN 0-582-89308-9

Printed in Great Britain
by Blantyre Printing Co. Ltd., Blantyre

Author: Wolfgang Lippert
Picture acknowledgements: Bellman 30; Bormann 9; Danesch 1
Eigstler 22; Eisenbeiss 13, 15; Esser 11, 12, 37, 44, 63, 77; Grein
u. Meyer 17; Harms 19; Kohlhaupt 50, 69; P Lippert 58, 66; W
Lippert 48, 70; Lippoldmüller 34, 67; Pott 23, 29, 64, 68, 73;
Reinhard 18; Ruckstuhl 51, 53; Sammer 24; Seidl 52; Singer 54
Scherz 36, 78; Schimmitat 26, 28, 31, 41, 49, 59; Wothe 20, 2
23, 32, 35, 40, 42, 43, 45, 46, 47, 55, 57, 60, 62, 65, 71, 75.

Foreword

This is a brief guide to the flowers of meadows and grasslands. It includes flowers that grow over much of western
Europe. Most of these are flowers that grow in Britain, but
some of them are much rarer here than on parts of the con-
tinent, or have a very limited range in Britain. A few of the
flowers cannot be seen growing wild in Britain, but may be
seen in cultivation, or may attract attention on a
continental holiday.

Only grassland flowers are included, although some kinds
may be found in other habitats too, such as woodland edges
or sparse woods where plenty of light reaches the ground.
Britain lacks some of the types of grassland seen on the con-
tinent, such as alpine meadows, and many of the grassland
types that do occur have been altered in recent years in
ways that do not suit the flowers. The very word meadow,
which used to conjure up a vision of a profusion of wild
flowers, is now itself becoming a rarity, as fewer and fewer
farms contain anything which could truthfully be termed a
meadow. There are still many places, however, where it is
possible to find an abundance of wild flowers. Anyone who
starts looking for flowers will soon realise that many of
them are rather precise in their requirements, and will grow
or flourish only where these are met. Grassland may be wet
or dry; acid, basic or neutral; sunny or shady; highland or
lowland; heavily-used for grazing, or used very little. All
these factors, and others too, may determine the mix of
plants found at a particular site.

Whether you go out on expeditions into the countryside
with the special aim of looking for plants, or whether you
are simply fond of rambling and identifying the plants that
you meet, this guide is for you. The book is made in a for-
mat which is easy to slip into the pocket and take with you.
It is nearly always easier identifying a plant *in situ* than by
trying to remember its appearance later. Taking home a
sample of flower or leaf is a poor answer, as it partially de-
stroys the very thing in which you are interested. With the
help of this book you should be able to recognise many

flowers, and at least identify the family to which others
belong.

Conservation

Many of Britain's flowers have decreased in recent years.
Some of the decrease is due to changes in farming methods.
Weedkillers have decreased the variety of plants. So, sometimes, have fertilisers, which tend to encourage the strong-
est-growing species at the expense of variety. Many flowers
have disappeared under buildings and roads as housing
spreads across the countryside. Still other plants have suf-
fered through overpicking, or simply from remorselessly
tramping feet.

Some of these causes may be beyond the power of the individual to alter, but there are ways of helping to conserve
flowers. Try not to trample on plants or damage the habitat.
Collect photographs rather than flowers. Plants are covered
by the Conservation of Wild Creatures and Wild Plants Act
1975, which makes it illegal to uproot plants without the
express permission of the owner of the land on which they
grow. Certain rare plants may not have any part, including
their seeds, collected.

It is also possible to grow 'wild' flowers in the garden.
Nowadays you can obtain the seeds of many species in
packets, just like the seeds of garden flowers. Given a little
thought, it may be possible to turn part of the garden into a
miniature hay meadow or chalk down of your own, and
help preserve part of our wild flower heritage.

Grassland habitats

The natural vegetation of much of Britain is woodland.
'Natural' grassland is probably confined to mountains
above the tree line, and some coastal and limestone areas.
Most of the rest of our grasslands have been created by
humans as they gradually cleared the woodlands, a process

which began way back in prehistoric times on the light soils of chalk and limestone hills and only later spread to the clay soils of the river valleys. Nowadays there is a whole variety of grassland habitats.

Water meadows, subject to periodic flooding, and used, if at all, for grazing, may occur near rivers. Undisturbed meadows may hold a varied collection of plants. Some flowers prefer a drier situation but dry meadows are now a rarity, usually being taken over for crop growing or intensive pasture. In some places, though, hay meadows remain where the grass and other plants are allowed to grow undisturbed through the early summer before being cut for hay. These meadows contain some of the best displays of real country flowers. Even heavily-used pasture land may still retain some of the native flowers.

Arable land is less good for the flower hunter. Modern agriculture, with its efficient weedkillers that selectively kill species unwanted by the farmer, and its techniques for 'cleaning' seed stocks of unwanted intruders, has grievously harmed the old variety of 'weeds' that used to be found on farms. But there are still corners and edges of fields where the wild flowers manage to survive. Indeed, some farmers deliberately leave such areas where they do not interfere with the efficiency of the harvest.

The hedgerows between fields and at the edges of roads also provide a strip of grassland habitat. In some places hedges have been ruthlessly grubbed up to make bigger fields, or the hedgerow has been sprayed with weedkiller, but where this does not happen the hedgerow flowers can still be seen through spring and summer.

A special type of grassland is seen on chalk. A thin dry soil and pressure from grazing may not seem a great recipe for producing flowers, but in fact the open grasslands of the downs with their basic soils provide a home for some of our most beautiful and interesting flowers. Further north, limestone country also has interesting flowers, some of which are the same as those of chalk. Chalk is famous, amongst other things, for its orchids and bellflowers. Many low-growing rosette plants thrive here.

Heathland is another habitat produced by man's activities. Some patches of grass and grassland flowers may occur mixed in with the heath vegetation.

'Wasteland' may not be wasted as far as flowers go. Many species make a good living here, and 'weed' species may also invade gardens and playing fields, some even thriving in that oddest type of grassland, the lawn. Some man-made habitats are even providing new opportunities for flowers – for example, the ever-increasing green ribbon of the motorway verges.

How to use this book

Most of the book is devoted to photographs in natural colours of flowers of Europe, together with brief descriptions of the species and their habits. Technical terms have been kept to a minimum, and those that do occur are explained in the glossary at the back of the book and the line drawings on the inside of the back cover.

The **species descriptions** each contain the following information:

Immediately below the photograph is the **common English name** of the flower. Many flowers have dozens of different names in different parts of the country, and many people have their own favourite dialect or old country name. The name given here, however, is the common name in widespread use, which would be recognised by most people. In a small number of cases more than one name may be widespread, and an alternative name is given at the end of the entry. Apart from this, the multiplicity of common names is ignored, not least because the same name was often given to several different plants, leading to confusion.

Underneath the English name is the **scientific name** of the species in *italics*. This consists of two parts. The first name, the genus name, has a capital letter. This name is shared with close relations – for example, the Bell-flowers are *Campanula.* The second name, the species name, starting with a small letter, identifies the species within the genus. Sometimes a third name is used to identify a subspecies or geographical variety, but these have not been used in this book.

To the right of the scientific name is given the **family** to which the species belongs, both in English (e.g. Cabbage family) and in scientific Latin (e.g. Cruciferae). The text below describes the **appearance** of the plant, including size, colour of the flower, arrangement of the flowers, shape and size of the leaves and which part of the plant they grow from, and so on. Some of these features are rather variable. For example, the height of a flower may depend to a certain extent on the conditions where it is growing, whether they are good or barely tolerable for the species. It may also depend on whether the grassland is mown or grazed – a daisy on a lawn is hardly likely to reach the maximum size for the species. Some plants also grow differently in different parts of their geographical range. Where a species is particularly variable this is noted.

The **habitat** of the plant is also noted, whether it prefers damp meadows or dry hill slopes, whether it extends to other habitats apart from grassland, and so on. Once again there may be variations. A plant may grow on low ground in northern Europe, but may be characteristic of mountain meadows further south.

The **distribution** of the plant is given, showing which parts of Europe you would expect to see it in, and whether it occurs in Britain. In many cases the flower will be seen only in parts of the countries mentioned – where the habitat is suitable – and may not even be present in all of these.

At the end of the flower description an **alternative name** may be noted, and there may be short **notes** on a particular feature of the plant, such as its edibility or poisonous nature, or whether it has or had use in medicine.

Below the text is a coloured stripe. Within this stripe you will find the months which make up the **flowering time** for the particular species. Flowering times may vary with many factors. Climate varies throughout Europe, and the flowering times in different countries may not correspond. Weather varies from year to year in the same place, and so may flowering times. So the flowering time given within the stripe is a wide one, spanning times when the flower may be seen in bloom somewhere in Europe. It is extremely unlikely to be seen in flower outside these times. The normal flowering time in Britain is usually much more restricted than this, the main flowering times may be noted in the text under 'Appearance'. Such notes always refer to Britain unless the flower does not occur here:

These flowers are rare or endangered

These flowers are not considered endangered species

Autumn Crocus

Colchicum autumnale
Lily family (Liliaceae)

Appearance: A rosy-mauve flower, occasionally white, autumn-flowering. Six-'petalled', growing from ground level on a weak stalk consisting of the flower tube. Up to 25cm high. No leaves at flowering time. Lanceolate leaves appear in spring, die down in summer. Below ground there is a large corm, up to 5cm. **Habitat:** Damp meadows. **Distribution:** Most of Europe except the north. Found in Britain. Also cultivated. **Notes:** Not a true crocus. Corms and seeds contain a poison, colchicine, used in experiments on cell division. **Alternative names:** Naked Ladies, Meadow Saffron.

German Wild Garlic

Allium suaveolens
Lily family (Liliaceae)

Appearance: Up to 60cm high. Globe-shaped flower-heads with a large number of flowers in a tight umbel. Petals are usually pink, with darker stripes down the middle, but can be paler or purplish. The flower parts are all in threes. The stamens protrude from the individual bell-shaped flowers. Flower-head held on a long leafless stalk. Leaves narrow, grasslike, and all grow from ground. **Habitat:** Damp meadows and woodland edges. **Distribution:** Scattered through central and southern Europe. Found in southern Germany. Does not occur in Britain.

Siberian Iris

Iris sibirica
Iris family (Iridaceae)

Appearance: Up to 100cm high. Bluish-purple flowers, the turned-out parts of the outer petals strongly veined with darker purple. A brown sheath to the flower head. Blooms are about 6cm across. Narrow leaves on slender stems, may be 2 to 5 flowers on one stem. **Habitat:** Grassy places in pastures and heaths. **Distribution:** Central Europe to Japan. Not native to Britain. It is, however, often planted in gardens, and there are various 'improved' varieties with colours ranging from white to deep purple. Some flower earlier than the wild form.

Pheasant's-eye Narcissus

Narcissus poeticus
Daffodil family (Amaryllidaceae)

Appearance: Six white petals and a short yellow trumpet at the centre of the flower. The margin of the trumpet is wavy and red. Medium-tall, at about 60cm. The leaves are narrow and grey-green. The flower head is somewhat nodding and is backed by a brown papery sheath. **Habitat:** Damp meadows, grassy places. **Distribution:** Originally a Mediterranean species, but introduced and now wild in central Europe. Cultivated in Britain and sometimes seen wild as an escape. **Notes:** The flowers of this species are sweetly scented.

Green-winged Orchid

Orchis morio
Orchid family (Orchidaceae)

Appearance: Rather variable in height, but can be as tall as 40cm. Flowers usually a rather reddish purple, but can be paler or even white. Several flowers on one short spike. The upper part of each flower, the hood, is formed from the sepals and has the conspicuous green veins which give this orchid its name. The leaves are lanceolate and green, without spots. Flowers mainly in May and June. **Habitat:** Grassland, meadows, open downland scrub. **Distribution:** Found over most of Europe, including Britain. Sometimes numerous in a suitable place. **Notes:** Fragrant.

Burnt Orchid

Orchis ustulata
Orchid family (Orchidaceae)

Appearance: Up to 30cm high. The flower-spike starts as a conical cluster with the buds a dark brownish maroon, giving a 'burnt' appearance. As the flowers open they become paler. The hood remains reddish but the lip below is 4-lobed and white with a few large pink dots. The leaves are rather oblong but have pointed tips. The main flowering time is May and June. **Habitat:** Dry grasslands, especially on lime; mountain meadows. **Distribution:** Found throughout most of Europe but absent from some northern parts. Occurs in Britain. **Notes:** Fragrant.

Broad-leaved Marsh Orchid

Dactylorhiza majalis
Orchid family (Orchidaceae)

Appearance: Quite tall, can be 50cm or more. Flowers are reddish-purple in a short dense spike. Lip 3-lobed, often with dark lines, and the hood has two narrow wings. The leaves are rather broad and bluish-green, typically strongly spotted with purplish blotches, although sometimes these are lacking. **Habitat:** Damp meadows, marshes, likes lime. **Distribution:** Found throughout Europe except the extreme north and south. Occurs in Britain.

Military Orchid

Orchis militaris
Orchid family (Orchidaceae)

Appearance: Up to 45cm, often shorter. Flowers in a large spike. Pink, sometimes with a greyish cast. Leaves rather large, oblong-oval, shiny, not spotted. Individual flowers have a hood, below which is a 5-lobed lip. The two lobes nearest the stalk form short thin 'arms', then two larger lobes form 'legs', with a tiny lobe between. The effect is of a tiny man, or soldier, giving the orchid its name. **Habitat:** Dry grassland, often on lime, also scrubland and woodland edges. **Distribution:** Widespread in Europe but absent or rare in many areas. Rare in Britain.

Fly Orchid

Ophrys insectifera
Orchid family (Orchidaceae)

Appearance: Up to 60cm, often less. Flowers not in dense spike but at intervals up the flowering stem. Individual flowers rather small. Sepals form 3-lobed green hood, below which are velvety, brownish-purple petals, with a shiny bluish patch in the middle. These form an imitation 'fly', with 'antennae'. The function of such imitations seems to be to induce an insect to attempt mating and so effect pollination. Flowers mainly in May and June. **Habitat:** Woodland edges, dry grassland, often on chalk. **Distribution:** Throughout Europe, rather local in Britain.

Bistort

Polygonum bistorta
Dock family (Polygonaceae)

Appearance: Up to 100cm high, usually much less. Flowers in a dense spike up to 7cm long, light pink. When fully open the spike is surrounded by a 'fuzz' of protruding stamens and styles. Close to, the flowers can be seen in pairs, one male, one female. Flowers mainly May to August. The leaves are smooth, quite large, some-what triangular, stalks sheathing the stem. **Habitat:** Damp meadows, verges, grassy wasteland. **Distribution:** Much of Europe, but confined to mountains in south. A common 'weed'. **Notes:** Used by herbalists. The leaves can be used in cooking.

Ragged Robin

Lychnis flos-cuculi
Pink family (Caryophyllaceae)

Appearance: Up to 90cm with a rough branched stem carrying the flowers. The flowers are pink, occasionally white, and have a ragged appearance due to the deeply cut petals, each of which has 4 not very regular lobes. Below the petals, the sepals form a long brownish tube. The upper leaves are narrow lanceolate, the basal leaves wider and spreading. Non-flowering stems occur among the flowering. Main season of flowering May and June. **Habitat:** Damp meadows, marshes, sometimes damp woodland. **Distribution:** Throughout Europe, including Britain.

Maiden Pink

Dianthus deltoides
Pink family (Caryophyllaceae)

Appearance: Up to 45cm high, often only 20cm. Delicate pink 5-petalled flowers, a few on each stalk. A long brown-green sepal tube, the bottom half enclosed by two scales. The plant forms loose tufts, with very narrow leaves, often rather greyish-green. Upper leaves pointed, but lower ones have rounded tips. Flowers from June to September. Flowers close up when the sky is overcast. **Habitat:** Dry banks, grassy places, especially where sandy. **Distribution:** Throughout Europe, including Britain, but not common here as wild plant. Frequently cultivated.

Bladder Campion

Silene vulgaris
Pink family (Caryophyllaceae)

Appearance: Up to 60cm high. The flowers are white, in loose clusters at the top of the stalk. The flowers nod, and there is, behind the rather small 2-lobed petals, the 'bladder' that gives this plant its name, made up of a bulging tube of sepals, brownish in colour and strongly veined. The leaves are oval with pointed tips, and may have a rather wavy edge. **Habitat:** Arable land, waste places, grassy places on lime, mountain pastures. **Distribution:** Throughout Europe, but varying slightly in different areas. In Britain it is commoner in the south.

Pasque Flower

Pulsatilla vulgaris
Buttercup family (Ranunculaceae)

Appearance: Large bell-shaped purple flowers up to 8cm across, with 5 petals and a bright yellow centre. Start erect, droop later. Occasional white or reddish flowers. The stem and the young leaves covered with silvery hair. Leaves much dissected, feathery. A low plant, 30cm or less. The main flowering season is in April and May. **Habitat:** Dry grassland on lime. **Distribution:** Mainly central Europe. Occurs in Britain but is rare. Found on dry chalky soil in the Chilterns and some other areas just north of the Thames. **Notes:** Poisonous, formerly used medicinally.

Yellow Adonis

Adonis vernalis
Buttercup family (Ranunculaceae)

Appearance: Large, showy, bright yellow flowers up to 8cm across, the 10–20 narrow elliptical petals opening to a flat plate. Scaly flower stems. Leaves are much dissected, feathery. Smooth stems. Rather short, never more than 40cm high. Flowers in April and May. **Habitat:** Dry grassland, rocky places, light pinewoods, on lime or sandy soil. **Distribution:** From Spain to southern Scandinavia, through southern Europe into Russia. Not found in Britain. **Notes:** Poisonous, but has been used medicinally.

Meadow Buttercup

Ranunculus acris
Buttercup family (Ranunculaceae)

Appearance: Tall, up to 90cm high. The flowers are bright yellow, each individual with its own stalk, but several may form a small cluster from one stem. 5-petalled, each petal with the outer edge nearly flat but with a slight indentation. Leaves divided into 2–7 lobes, the end lobe unstalked. The lobes have a jagged edge but a rounded total outline. Often occurs in large numbers, carpeting the ground. Main flowering from May to July. **Habitat:** Damp meadows. **Distribution:** Throughout Europe, including Britain. Common meadow weed. **Notes:** Poisonous to cattle.

Marsh Marigold

Caltha palustris
Buttercup family (Ranunculaceae)

Appearance: Large golden-yellow 5-petalled flowers up to 5cm across, but in some areas are much smaller. The middle of the flower has up to 100 yellow stamens. Flowers mainly March to June. The leaves are large and heart-shaped, with toothed edges. They are deep green and glossy. The upper ones on the stem are stalkless, the lower ones have long stems. On high ground the stems sprawl and the flowers are small. **Habitat:** Mainly marshes, wet woods, ditches and fens. **Distribution:** Throughout Europe, including Britain. **Notes:** Poisonous to cattle. **Alternative name:** Kingcup.

Globe Flower

Trollius europaeus
Buttercup family (Ranunculaceae)

Appearance: Up to 70cm high. The flower is pale yellow, sometimes with a green tinge, up to 5cm across. 10 rounded incurved sepals make up the rounded bloom, which is carried on a long stalk. The dark green leaves have 3 to 5 main lobes, each of them further divided. Upper leaves have no stalk. Flowers mainly from June to August. **Habitat:** Wet pastures, scrub and thickets, usually in upland areas. **Distribution:** Throughout much of Europe. In Britain in the mountain areas of the west and north. **Notes:** Poisonous.

Lady's Smock

Cardamine pratensis
Cabbage family (Brassicaceae)

Appearance: Up to 60cm high, often less. Flowers are in a small dense cluster at the top of the stem, each flower 1.5–2cm across. Colour rather variable: usually pale lilac-pink, but may be any shade from white to violet. 4 petals, short sepals. Leaves at the base form a rosette and differ in shape from those on the stem. All are made up of leaflets, kidney-shaped ones on the basal leaves, pointed on the stem. **Habitat:** Damp meadows, and near streams. **Distribution:** Throughout Europe, including Britain. **Alternative name:** Cuckooflower.

Meadow Saxifrage

Saxifraga granulata
Saxifrage family (Saxifragaceae)

Appearance: Single-stemmed, up to 50cm high. A few white flowers, up to 2cm across, in a loose cluster at the top of the stem. 5 petals. A few small leaves on the stem, most of the lobed, kidney-shaped leaves near the base, on long stalks. Many small brown bulbils at the base of the plant. **Habitat:** Dry meadows, dry rocky places, light woodland, on well-drained soil. **Distribution:** Scattered throughout most of Europe, but scarce in some areas. In Britain chiefly in east, but overall less common than it was.

Great Burnet

Sanguisorba officinalis
Rose family (Rosaceae)

Appearance: Up to 90cm high, the flower-heads deep blood-red, on long stalks. The flower-head 1–2cm long, oval, with many tiny flowers packed in, each with no petals, but 4 red sepals. Leaves are pinnate, with 7 to 15 pairs of deeply toothed leaflets, dark green above, greyish below. **Habitat:** Damp grassland. **Distribution:** Throughout most of Europe. In Britain it is found mostly in central England and Wales. **Notes:** Formerly used medicinally to staunch the flow of blood – hence *Sanguisorba*, meaning blood-absorbing.

Red-stalked Cinquefoil

Potentilla heptaphylla
Rose family (Rosaceae)

Appearance: Very variable. Up to 20cm high, a prostrate plant with creeping stems that does not form mats. Flowers are numerous, have 5 golden-yellow petals, and are up to 1cm across. The flowering stems are reddish. Sepals green, oval, shorter than the petals. The basal leaves are divided into 5 to 7 leaflets, and have long stalks. The upper leaves are smaller, less divided, with shorter stalks. **Habitat:** Dry grassland, scrub and light woodland, especially on chalk. **Distribution:** Central Europe north to southern Scandinavia. Does not occur in Britain.

Black Medick

Medicago lupulina
Pea family (Leguminosae)

Appearance: Up to 50cm, but more often a low, spreading plant. Tiny yellow flowers in a rounded head up to 0.8cm long. There can be from 10 to 50 flowers in a head. The leaves have three leaflets, each nearly oval, but wider towards the end. The rounded tip of the leaflet has a small sharp point in the middle. The plant is usually downy. Flowers mainly from May to August. **Habitat:** Waste places, fields, roadsides. **Distribution:** Throughout Europe, including Britain, especially the south-east. **Notes:** Cultivated in some places as animal fodder.

Kidney Vetch

Anthyllis vulneraria
Pea family (Leguminosae)

Appearance: Very variable. Up to 50cm high. Flowers in dense heads, rather flat below, surrounded by a 'dish' of bracts. Flower-heads often in pairs. Flowers often yellow, but can also be orange, red, or purple, sometimes nearly white. The sepals are woolly and enclose the lower part of the petal tube. Leaves with 3–13 leaflets, the one at the tip largest. Stems and leaves are silky. Flowers mainly from June to September. **Habitat:** Dry grassland, especially on downland, near the sea or on mountains. **Distribution:** Throughout Europe, including Britain.

Sainfoin

Onobrychis viciifolia
ea family (Leguminosae)

Appearance: Up to 80cm high, fairly erect. Flowers are bright magenta pink, with darker veining. In clusters of up to 50 in a spike at the top of the stalk, lower flowers opening before the upper. The leaves are large, but divided into from 13 to 25 leaflets. Flowers mainly from June to August. **Habitat:** Grassy banks, waste places. In Britain especially on chalk and limestone. **Distribution:** Central European in origin, but has been widely introduced and cultivated for use as cattle fodder, and is now found wild throughout much of Europe.

Horseshoe Vetch

Hippocrepis comosa
Pea family (Leguminosae)

Appearance: Rarely more than 20cm high, with a prostrate, spreading habit, but can be up to 40cm. Golden-yellow flowers, 5–12 in a head, in a compact group at the end of a stalk, each up to 1cm long. The leaves are made up of from 9 to 31 leaflets. Hairless. Flowers mainly May to July. **Habitat:** Dry grassland, banks, grassy cliffs. **Distribution:** Throughout much of Europe, except the north. Occurs in Britain mainly on limestone and chalk soils. **Notes:** The name comes from the shape of the seed-pods, which break up into horseshoe-like segments when ripe.

Bird's-foot Trefoil

Lotus corniculatus
Pea family (Leguminosae)

Appearance: Up to 40cm, but usually less. Spreading and prostrate. Flowers are yellow, carried in stalked heads with from 2 to 7 in each. Each flower is up to 1.5cm long, and often streaked with red. The leaves have 5 leaflets, but the lowest 2 are so close to the stem that to the casual glance there seem to be only 3 leaflets. Hairless. Flowers mainly June to September. **Habitat:** Dry grassland, roadsides, fields. **Distribution:** Throughout Europe, including Britain. **Notes:** The name comes from the straight seed pods that stick out like a bird's toes.

White Clover

Trifolium repens
Pea family (Leguminosae)

Appearance: Up to 30cm high, but usually lower, creeping across the ground. Flowers in neat globular flower-heads on long stalks. Flowers white, sometimes pink, the heads up to 3cm across, drooping and going brown after flowering. Each leaf has 3 equal leaflets, their bases close together and with a light whitish band in a semicircle near the base. Hairless. Flowers mainly June to September. **Habitat:** Grassy places, roadsides, fields, likes clay soils. **Distribution:** Throughout Europe, including Britain. Often cultivated, especially as an addition to grass in pasture land for cattle. A tough weed in lawns.

Red Clover

Trifolium pratense
Pea family (Leguminosae)

Appearance: Up to 60cm high when growing erect, but often with a more spreading habit. Flower-heads may be globular, but often rather egg-shaped, reddish-purple in colour rather than red, sometimes cream. Flower-heads immediately above top leaves on the stem, no stalk. Leaflets 3 to a leaf, rather pointed. A pale V on each leaflet. Somewhat hairy. Flowers mainly May to September. **Habitat:** Grassy places, pastures, roadsides. **Distribution:** Throughout Europe, including Britain. It is widely cultivated in pastures as it is a good fodder plant for cattle.

Lesser Yellow Trefoil

Trifolium dubium
Pea family (Leguminosae)

Appearance: Usually low-growing, but occasionally up to 50cm high. Yellow flower-heads on stalks growing from the junction of stem and leaf. Each flower-head has 10 to 25 flowers, but only reaches 0.7cm across. Heads turn brown as they fruit. The leaves have 3 leaflets, which are wider towards the rounded tip. Leaflets up to 1cm long, the middle one the longest. Somewhat downy.
Habitat: Grassy places, banks, pastures, roadsides. **Distribution:** Throughout Europe, including Britain, but rarer in the north of Britain than the south.

Bush Vetch

Vicia sepium
Pea family (Leguminosae)

Appearance: A scrambling, sprawling plant up to 100cm high.
Flowers are pale purple, and in a short spike with up to 6 flowers
and a very short stalk. Each flower up to 1.5cm long. The leaves
have 5 to 9 pairs of leaflets and end in a branching tendril which
helps the plant to scramble. The plant is fairly smooth. Main
flowering time from May to August. **Habitat:** Grassy places, hedges,
thickets, and as a weed in gardens. **Distribution:** Throughout
Europe, including Britain, where it is common.

Meadow Vetchling

Lathyrus pratensis
Pea family (Leguminosae)

Appearance: Scrambling, climbing plant up to 120cm tall. Yellow flowers, each up to 2cm long, in clusters of from 5 to 12, on long strong stalks. Each leaf has 2 lanceolate leaflets, and 2 leafy stipules where it joins the stem. Leaves end in tendrils, which may or may not be branched. The stems have a square cross-section with sharply angled corners, but are rather weak and are supported by one another and surrounding plants. **Habitat:** Grassy places, roadside banks and hedges. **Distribution:** Throughout Europe including Britain.

Cypress Spurge

Euphorbia cyparissias
Spurge family (Euphorbiaceae)

Appearance: Non-flowering stems have straight narrow yellowish-green leaves which stick out sideways, looking like a small conifer, and giving this plant its name. Flowering stems end in a head with 9–15 branches on which are the flowers, the obvious parts of which are yellow kidney-shaped bracts which sometimes turn red. Leaves are narrow and numerous. The upright stems are linked below ground by stolons. **Habitat:** Bare places, wasteland, grassy places, cultivated ground. **Distribution:** Throughout Europe but may have been introduced to Britain and Scandinavia.

Meadow Cranesbill

Geranium pratense
Geranium family (Geraniaceae)

Appearance: Up to 80cm high. Large violet-blue (or sometimes white or lilac) flowers, up to 3cm across, with 5 broad petals with round tips, small green sepals, and conspicuous black-tipped stamens. Leaves are cut, almost to the base, into 5 to 7 lobes, the lobes themselves being deeply toothed. Lower leaves on long stalks, upper leaves close to stem. The plant is covered with dense soft hairs. **Habitat:** Damp meadows, near streams and ditches, grassy places. **Distribution:** Throughout most of Europe, locally common in Britain. Grown in gardens.

Perforate St. John's Wort

Hypericum perforatum
Hypericum family (Guttiferae)

Appearance: An erect plant up to 100cm high, often less. The flowers are yellow with black dots along the edge of the petals. Sepals may also have black dots. Flowers in branched clusters, each flower up to 2cm across. Leaves are hairless with translucent glandular dots, which give the appearance of holes, hence 'perforate'. The stem has 2 raised lines running down opposite sides. Flowers mainly June to September. **Habitat:** Open woods, grassland, banks, especially on lime. **Distribution:** Throughout most of Europe, including Britain, where it is rarer in the north.

Wild Pansy

Viola tricolor
Violet family (Violaceae)

Appearance: Up to 30cm high. Flowers with a flat face, and 5 petals, 4 'above', 1 below. Sepals are short. As the species name suggests, is often tricoloured, with violet, white and yellow, although some are mainly violet. A variable species, with several named variations. Those in the picture are from the mountains of central Europe. Leaves are heart-shaped to lanceolate. Flowers mainly from April to September. **Habitat:** Grassy places, dunes, waste and cultivated ground. **Distribution:** Throughout Europe, including Britain. **Alternative name:** Heartsease.

Astrantia

Astrantia major
Carrot family (Umbelliferae)

Appearance: Up to 70cm high. Flowers white or pinkish, with a feathery look, in dense umbels up to 5cm across. Surrounding bracts purplish-green above. Umbels carried on long slender stalks. The leaves are palmate, with 3 to 7 lobes, all coarsely toothed. Lower leaves on long stalks, up to 15cm across. Hairless. Main flowering time from June to September. **Habitat:** Woods, meadows, especially in mountains. **Distribution:** Through much of Europe, but not native to Britain, although it has become naturalised in several parts of the country. **Notes:** Sweet-smelling. **Alternative name:** Great Masterwort.

Cow Parsley

Anthriscus sylvestris
Carrot family (Umbelliferae)

Appearance: Up to 120cm high. White flowers in umbels up to 6cm across, each of these composed of 4 to 15 groups of little flowers. No bracts at the base of the umbels, but small ones beneath the flowers. Outer flowers have unequal petals. The leaves are up to 30cm long, subdivided 2 or 3 times into leaflets, somewhat hairy below. Stalks of the plant are hollow. Flowers mainly from April to June. **Habitat:** Hedges, roadsides, woodland edges, wasteland. **Distribution:** Throughout Europe, including Britain. **Notes:** Distinctive odour.

Hogweed

Heracleum sphondylium
Carrot family (Umbelliferae)

Appearance: Stout plant up to 200cm high, with stiff hairs. Flowers white or sometimes pink, and can be 15cm or more across. There are 7 to 20 divisions of the umbel, and the individual flowers are quite large, up to 1cm, the outer flowers being larger and having unequal petals. Leaves up to 60cm, divided into leaflets, each broad but deeply lobed. Stem thick, ridged and hollow. Flowers mainly June to September. **Habitat:** Grassy places, woods, hedges, roadsides. **Distribution:** All of Europe, including Britain. **Notes:** Formerly fed to pigs. Unpleasant scent. **Alternative name:** Cow Parsnip.

Caraway

Carum carvi
Carrot family (Umbelliferae)

Appearance: Up to 60cm high, much branched, with rather small and irregular umbels of white flowers, each up to 4cm across. Each umbel has 5 to 10 divisions. Flowering heads look rather thin. Leaves somewhat filmy-looking, as they are divided into leaflets, these are divided again, and then the lobes are deeply cut into narrow segments. Flowers mainly June and July. **Habitat:** Meadows, mountain woods, waste places. **Distribution:** Throughout most of Europe. In Britain probably introduced; rare and scattered. **Notes:** Source of aromatic caraway seeds. Cultivated.

Cowslip

Primula veris
Primrose family (Primulaceae)

Appearance: Up to 30cm, may be much lower in pasture. Deep yellow flowers, up to 30 of them in a head at the top of a stem. The flowers droop, have a long yellowish-green tube formed by the sepals, and the petals are only 1–1.5cm across. There is an orange spot at the base of the petal lobe. The leaves grow from the ground as a rosette. They are deeply wrinkled, somewhat toothed, and are broad towards the tip but abruptly narrowed at the base. **Habitat:** Meadows, grassland, scrub, especially on lime or downland. **Distribution:** Throughout Europe. In Britain rarer in north.

Cross Gentian

Gentiana cruciata
Gentian family (Gentianaceae)

Appearance: Up to 50cm high, rather leafy. Flowers are dull purple-blue, in clusters at the top of a stem or arising from where leaves branch from the stem. Each flower a 5-petalled bell up to 2.5cm long. Leaves are large, up to 10cm, rather leathery and oval or broad lanceolate. Flowers mainly July to September. **Habitat:** Dry meadows, rocky places, open woods. **Distribution:** Central and south-eastern Europe. Does not occur in Britain.

Chiltern Gentian

Gentianella germanica
Gentian family (Gentianaceae)

Appearance: Up to 50cm high, but usually less. Flowers are bright bluish-mauve, from a few to many in a head. The flowers are large, up to 3.5cm long, and have 5 petals formed into a tube for part of their length, with green sepals outside only half the length. Leaves oval to lanceolate. Basal leaves differ, but are usually dead by flowering. Flowers mainly September and October. **Habitat:** Meadows, pastures, dry grassland and scrub on chalk. **Distribution:** Western and central Europe. Rare and local in Britain from Hampshire to Bedford.

Fringed Gentian

Gentianella ciliata
Gentian family (Gentianaceae)

Appearance: Up to 25cm high, with slender bending stems. Large blue flowers, up to 5cm across, with 4 large petal lobes spreading from the end of the flower tube. The edges of these lobes carry a conspicuous fringe of blue hairs. The flowers are on long stalks, and 2 to 5 arise from where the upper leaves join the stem. Leaves are rather straight, only 3–4cm long. **Habitat:** Dry meadows, light woodland, rocky places. **Distribution:** Mainly central and southern Europe, but reaches into France and Belgium. Does not occur in Britain.

Blue Bugle

Ajuga genevensis
Mint family (Labiatae)

Appearance: Up to 40cm high, often much less. Flowers deep bright blue, or very occasionally pink, in a long rather loose spike in which the bracts are usually tinted blue. The sepals are hairy, and the stamens project. The basal leaves are up to 12cm long, but usually die before flowers appear. Stem leaves also large, oblong and hairy. Flowers mainly May to July. **Habitat:** Dry grassy places, rocky and stony places, screes, dunes. **Distribution:** Mainly in central and south-east Europe; not native to Britain, but living as an introduction in a few localities.

Meadow Clary

Salvia pratensis
Mint family (Labiatae)

Appearance: Up to 100cm high. Flowers bright violet-blue, occasionally white or pink, in whorls on a long spike. The whorls are spaced out and the spike has no leaves. Each flower up to 2.5cm. Most leaves grow from the base and are broad to lanceolate, with a somewhat toothed edge. The few leaves on the stem are narrow and stalkless. The plant is hairy, the hairs being glandular and producing a sticky secretion. Flowers mainly June and July. **Habitat:** Meadows, grassy places, roadsides. **Distribution:** Throughout Europe. In Britain a rare plant of southern chalk districts.

Large Self-heal

Prunella grandiflora
Mint family (Labiatae)

Appearance: Up to 40cm high. Flowers in dense clusters at the top of the stem, a bright violet. Each flower up to 2.5cm long, the lower part tubular, the upper opening out with the upper lip forming a hood above the lower. Bracts often purplish. The leaves are up to 5cm long, oval and scarcely toothed. **Habitat:** Dry grassland, bare ground. **Distribution:** Throughout most of Europe except the extreme west. Not found in Britain, where the smaller-flowered Common Self-heal (*Prunella vulgaris*) is widespread.

Eyebright

Euphrasia rostkoviana
Figwort family (Scrophulariaceae)

Appearance: Up to 30cm high. Two-lipped flowers. Lower lip conspicuously striped with purple over the white background and the orange-yellow blotch on the lip. Upper lip is mainly lilac inside and has lilac stripes on the outside. Each flower up to 1cm long, with others in a small cluster at the top of a stem. Leaves are small, bright green, and toothed, with a dense covering of glandular hairs. Flowers mainly July and August. **Habitat:** Dry meadows, pastures, open woods. **Distribution:** Throughout most of Europe, including Britain. **Notes:** A semi-parasite.

Yellow Rattle

Rhinanthus minor
Figwort family (Scrophulariaceae)

Appearance: Rather variable, up to 80cm high. Yellow flowers in small groups at the top of a stem. Two-lipped, the upper lip with a straight tube and two 'teeth' at the side, which are usually violet. The sepals are fused and form a rounded bowl for the base of the flower and then the fruit, the seeds inside which form the rattle that gives the plant its name. Leaves are narrow, rough and toothed. Stem usually black-spotted. **Habitat:** Grassy places, meadows, cornfields. **Distribution:** Throughout most of Europe, including Britain. **Notes:** A semi-parasite.

Slender Speedwell

Veronica filiformis
Figwort family (Scrophulariaceae)

Appearance: A hairy plant with many creeping stems. Flowers up to 1.5cm across, bright purplish-blue, the lower lobe sometimes lighter. Centre of flower yellow-white. Two long stamens protrude, and the style. Flowers are on very long stalks. Stems are very slender and form mats. Leaves are kidney-shaped with a toothed margin, and have short stalks. Flowers mainly from April to June.
Habitat: Grassy places, roadsides, cultivated ground, lawns. **Distribution:** Originally from Asia Minor, but widely naturalised in Europe, including Britain.

Germander Speedwell

Veronica chamaedrys
Figwort family (Scrophulariaceae)

Appearance: Up to 40cm high, often less. Flowers bright powder-blue with a white centre, about 1cm across, the lowest of the four petals the smallest. The style and stamen filaments are also blue, anthers white. From 10 to 20 flowers in a cluster on a long stalk growing from the point where a leaf branches from the stem. Upward growing stems have white hairs in two lines on opposite sides. Leaves more or less oval, coarsely toothed. Flowers mainly March to July. **Habitat:** Grassy places, woods, hedges. **Distribution:** Throughout Europe, including Britain.

Ribwort Plantain

Plantago lanceolata
Plantain family (Plantaginaceae)

Appearance: Up to 40cm high. Flowering head carried on a long stalk which grows from the base of the plant. The flower spike is up to 2cm long, and contains many small flowers, each with 4 small brownish petals and 4 stamens that protrude well beyond the petals. The stamens are white or yellow. The leaves are up to 15cm long and lanceolate, long-stalked, with 3 to 5 strong veins, or ribs that give the plant its name. Flowers mainly April to August. **Habitat:** Meadows, roadsides, waste places, lawns. **Distribution:** Throughout Europe, including Britain.

Lady's Bedstraw

Galium verum
Bedstraw family (Rubiaceae)

Appearance: Up to 100cm, but often less, with stems that have many branches, some upright, some sprawling. Profuse clusters of small yellow flowers in heads at the tops of the branches. Each flower only 0.4cm or less across. Flower clusters are leafy, giving a greenish-yellow overall appearance to the heads. Stem square. Leaves linear, in whorls of 8 to 12. Flowers mainly in July and August. **Habitat:** Dry grassland, hedgerows, old sand dunes. **Distribution:** Throughout Europe, including Britain. **Notes:** Dyes can be made from the shoots and roots.

Hedge Bedstraw

Galium mollugo
Bedstraw family (Rubiaceae)

Appearance: Rather variable. Up to 120cm high, stems erect or straggling. Tiny white flowers only 0.4cm across in branching clusters at the top of the stem, the whole flower head having a rather thin appearance. Stems square. Leaves up to 2.5cm long, narrow or almost oval, with a single vein, and with prickles that project forward. The leaves are in whorls of 6 to 8 on the stem. Flowers mainly June to September. **Habitat:** Hedgerows, grassy and waste places, roadsides, open woodland, especially on lime soils. **Distribution:** Throughout Europe, including Britain.

Field Scabious

Knautia arvensis
Teasel family (Dipsacaceae)

Appearance: Up to 150cm high, with flower-heads of bluish-lilac. The heads are up to 4cm across, circular, flat below and slightly convex above. Each consists of up to 50 tiny flowers, all with four petals, but flowers to the outside of the disc are larger. Several flower-heads may branch from one stem, each on a long stalk. Lower leaves are undivided, but higher up the stem they become more and more cut into lobes. Flowers mainly July to September. **Habitat:** Dry grassland, pastures, banks and roadsides. **Distribution:** Throughout Europe, including Britain.

Clustered Bellflower

Campanula glomerata
Bellflower family (Campanulaceae)

Appearance: Up to 80cm high, but usually much lower. The flowers are violet or blue, sometimes white, and form a little tight cluster at the top of a stem. Individual flowers are up to 2cm long, have no stalk, and have 5 petals in the bell. Leaves are narrow oval to heart-shaped. Lower leaves have stalks, upper leaves without, and with the base wrapped around the stem. **Habitat:** Grassland, grassy roadsides, open woods, especially on lime. **Distribution:** Throughout Europe, including Britain. **Notes:** Sometimes cultivated, when may be larger than in the wild.

Spreading Bellflower

Campanula patula
Bellflower family (Campanulaceae)

Appearance: Up to 60cm high. Flowers pale blue-violet, with rather open bells and short petal tubes. Each flower up to 2.5cm long. Flowers in very loose clusters at the tops of stems, each flower on its own long thin stalk, usually with a small bract in the middle of the stalk. Lower leaves up to 4cm, oblong, with a stalk. Upper leaves narrow with no stalk. Flowers mainly July to August. **Habitat:** Grassland, hedges, woodland. **Distribution:** Throughout most of Europe. In Britain occurs scattered and locally in England and Wales.

Daisy

Bellis perennis
Daisy family (Compositae)

Appearance: Up to 15cm high. The leaves form rosettes on the ground, from which each flower-head grows on its own stalk. Each head 1.5–2.5cm across, and has a yellow centre surrounded by white rays, often tinged with pink at the ends. The yellow centre is made up of numerous little flowers, and each of the rays comprises another little flower. The flower stalk has hairs and no leaves. The leaves have oval tips, joined by a broad stalk to the rootstock. Main flowering from June to September. **Habitat:** Short grassland, lawns. **Distribution:** Throughout Europe, including Britain.

Yarrow

Achillea millefolium
Daisy family (Compositae)

Appearance: Up to 50cm high. Flat white flower-heads, subdivided into many branches, each little stalk holding what appears to be a 5-petalled flower. In fact each of these is made up of many central florets and 5 ray florets making the 'petals'. The leaves are divided into lobes, then these are divided and divided again, giving leaves with many tiny narrow lobes. Flowers mainly from June to August. **Habitat:** Meadows, banks, hedges, roadsides. **Distribution:** Throughout Europe, including Britain. **Notes:** Very strongly scented. **Alternative name:** Milfoil.

Michaelmas Daisy

Aster amellus
Daisy family (Compositae)

Appearance: Up to 60cm high. 'Flowers' made up of golden yellow central florets and long narrow bluish-lilac ray florets. Usually in a cluster of a few heads, sometimes single. Each head up to 5cm across. Leaves rather rough and hairy, the lower ones stalked, more or less oval, the upper ones without stalks and narrower. **Habitat:** Dry grassland, rocky places, scrub, open woods. **Distribution:** Originally central and south-east Europe. Not native to Britain. One of the species planted as garden Michaelmas Daisies, so seen in cultivation in most of Europe.

Arnica

Arnica montana
Daisy family (Compositae)

Appearance: Up to 60cm high. The flower-heads are bright orange-yellow, each up to 8cm across, with an orange centre and long ray florets. Each is on a separate stalk, with one or two pairs of small lanceolate leaves along its length. Larger lanceolate leaves covered with glandular hairs form a rosette at the base of the plant. Whole plant downy. **Habitat:** Grassy places, open woods, in hills and mountains. Flowers mainly June to August. **Distribution:** Central Europe to France and Denmark. Not found in Britain. **Notes:** Aromatic. Juices a remedy for sprains and bruises.

Ox-eye Daisy

Leucanthemum vulgare
Daisy family (Compositae)

Appearance: Up to 60cm high, sometimes more. Flower-heads are large white daisies with yellow centres. Each grows on its own stalk and is up to 5cm across. Upper leaves are narrow oblongs, deeply divided, with the base clasping the stem. The lower leaves are long-stalked and more rounded, somewhat toothed. Flowers mainly June to August. **Habitat:** Grassland of all types. **Distribution:** Throughout Europe, including Britain, where it is much less common in the north. **Alternative names:** Marguerite, Moon-daisy.

Brown-rayed Knapweed

Centaurea jacea
Daisy family (Compositae)

Appearance: Rather variable, branched plant up to 60cm high. Flower-heads up to 2cm across, shaped like a sweep's brush, with reddish-purple florets. Below these, bracts envelop the base of the flower-head, each brownish with a light margin. Several heads may branch off a single stem. Leaves are hairy, rather rough, lower ones with stalks, the upper ones smaller, narrower, stalkless. Flowers mainly August and September. **Habitat:** Grassy places, light woodland. **Distribution:** Most of Europe, but introduced in Britain, where it is sometimes found in the south.

Wig Knapweed

Centaurea phrygia
Daisy family (Compositae)

Appearance: Rather variable, up to 120cm high. Large red-purple flower-heads up to 6cm across when fully open. The bracts below the florets make a rather round base to the flower-head, and each has many bristles. Stems branch, with several flower-heads. Lower leaves oval, with a stalk. Upper leaves narrower, finely toothed at the margin. **Habitat:** Meadows, light woodland. **Distribution:** Found in slightly different forms throughout much of Europe from Scandinavia to eastern Europe and the Balkans. In mountains in the south. Does not occur in Britain.

Cabbage Thistle

Cirsium oleraceum
Daisy family (Compositae)

Appearance: Up to 120cm high, erect with a grooved stem. Flower-heads oval, up to 4cm long, with rather small yellowish-white florets, occasionally reddish. Flower-heads in small dense clusters, surrounded by short, broad, yellowish leaves. Main leaves yellow-ish-green, with bristles along the edge, sharply toothed but rather soft. Flowers mainly July and August. **Habitat:** Marshes, fens, wet meadows, beside water, in damp woods. **Distribution:** In most of Europe except far south and north. Not native to Britain, but introduced, and found in a few localities.

Stemless Thistle

Cirsium acaulon
Daisy family (Compositae)

Appearance: Usually right on the ground, rarely a stem grows to 30cm. Typically 1 (but up to 4) flower-head grows directly from the centre of the ground-hugging leaf rosette. Heads rather oval, up to 4cm long, with bright purple-red florets. The leaves are up to 15cm long and 3cm across, with wavy edges and many lobes, each lobe having 3 or 4 strong spines. **Habitat:** Dry pastures, especially where well-grazed, banks, roadsides. Typical of chalk. **Distribution:** Much of Europe, except Mediterranean area. In Britain found on chalk as far north as Yorkshire.

Rough Hawksbeard

Crepis biennis
Daisy family (Compositae)

Appearance: Tall, up to 120cm, with golden-yellow flower-heads up to 3.5cm across. Stems branched, thick, with flower-heads growing on hairy stalks, all to about the same height. The bracts enveloping the flower-head are hairy and glandular. Leaves are all rough with scattered hairs. Variable in shape, but more or less lanceolate and cut into lobes. Flowers mainly June and July. **Habitat:** Pastures, fields, roadsides, waste places. **Distribution:** Found throughout most of Europe, including Britain, where it is commonest in lowland areas with lime soils.

Common Catsear

Hypochoeris radicata
Daisy family (Compositae)

Appearance: Up to 60cm high. The bright yellow flower-heads, up to 4cm across, are carried on rather bare, sometimes branched, stems. Below the florets are bracts with bristles along their midribs. Each yellow floret has five teeth on the end of the petal tube. Leaves are up to 25cm long, with a wavy or toothed edge, and form a rosette at the base of the plant. Flowers mainly June to September.
Habitat: Dry pastures, roadsides, open woodland, grassy dunes. **Distribution:** Throughout Europe, including Britain. **Notes:** Has been used as salad or by herbalists.

Dandelion

Taraxacum officinale
Daisy family (Compositae)

Appearance: Very variable. Up to about 30cm, may be less. Familiar golden-yellow flower-heads, up to 5cm across, grow singly on long stalks from the base. Some of the bracts below the flower-head are usually curved back. The leaves are long, and more or less lanceolate, but they may vary from almost entire to deeply cut into triangular lobes. They all grow in a basal rosette. Flowers especially from April to June. **Habitat:** Grasslands of all kinds, roadsides and waste places, lawns. **Distribution:** Throughout Europe, including Britain. **Notes:** Leaves can be used in salads.

Goatsbeard

Tragopogon pratensis
Daisy family (Compositae)

Appearance: Up to 70cm high, with yellow flower-heads on top of the stems, which are not often branched. Long green bracts surround the head and are still conspicuous when flowers are fully out. Flowers open only in the morning. The stalk widens just below the flower-head. Plant rather blue-green. Leaves straplike, rather like a grass, their bases sheathing the stem. Flowers mainly June and July. **Habitat:** Meadows, pastures, banks, roadsides, dunes, waste places. **Distribution:** Throughout Europe, including Britain. **Alternative name:** Jack-go-to-bed-at-noon.